They Are Sick

by Jessica Quilty

PEARSON

Scott
Foresman

Editorial Offices: Glenview, Illinois • Parsippany, New Jersey • New York, New York
Sales Offices: Needham, Massachusetts • Duluth, Georgia • Glenview, Illinois
Coppell, Texas • Sacramento, California • Mesa, Arizona

ISBN: 0-328-13146-6

5 6 7 8 9 10 V010 14 13 12 11 10 09 08 07

Here is Pip.
Pip is sick.

Here is Bix.

Bix is sick.

Here is Vin.

Vin is sick.

Here is the vet.
The vet can fix up Pip,
Bix, and Vin.

Here is Tim.

Tim can take Vin back.

How to Be a Vet!

Read Together

Some people who like science and animals want to become vets. People go to school for many years to be vets. There are special schools that teach how to be a doctor for animals. There are thousands of vets in the United States!